I0756019

FINISHING LINE PRESS
www.finishinglinepress.com

Inept Love

poems by

HR Harper

Finishing Line Press
Georgetown, Kentucky

Inept Love

ISBN 979-8-89990-453-0 First Edition

ACKNOWLEDGMENTS

"Limited Supplies" and "The Longest Suffering" were published by *Written Tales Magazine*
"Before Winter" was published by *ANATE*
"The God of Gaps" was published by *Cathexis Northwest Press*

Publisher: Leah Huete de Maines
Editor: Christen Kincaid
Cover Art: Harper Family Archive
Author Photo: HR Harper
Cover Design: Elizabeth Maines McCleavy

Order online: www.finishinglinepress.com
also available on amazon.com

Author inquiries and mail orders:
Finishing Line Press
PO Box 1626
Georgetown, Kentucky 40324
USA

Contents

Limited Supplies

Finally I find
why wounds will
help. I put my hands
inside them, to
prove I am alive,
to verify the divine
in me until
it's exhausted
and then perhaps
I'll die in something
that looks like
prose, wrapped
in thin
white linen
as temporary
as skin.

Even doubt
has a beauty,
a purpose.

Meetings at the Edge

it's sundown in the small house in the forest
filling with smells of food

it's dinnertime and we set out the usual
with old anger that steepened today

so we climb the familiar unfair
as the shimmering ring of the triangle
calls us to suffering

you don't want to suffer
and you tell me to take new pity, to carry it away
though you give no hint where

so pity stays in its place, and its stoney fate weighs
on our best dinner plates—
our rock-red knuckles
try to save a shaken evening;
we put a finger on the scale of our cherished lies
and wait for clapping hands
then bow to the delusions we share

it's hard to swallow the argument of this particular air—
glossed with distance and grievance
and connubial contrivances strewn ahead
on this table hewn by broken bread
where the artifice of loss loosens
a luminous solitude

by such light
I wanted to empty you
I could not
I touch you to tell you
the habits of our lies sharpen the edges
that slice us open and raw to the darkened air—
it is here my fate finds your diamond sadness

what you wanted and could not have
pulled the curtains on this day with what that other
day left in you

*

our garden, unlike marriage
is fecund— huge zucchinis will not
stop growing. our garden
feeds us when we are not ready
with this food of earthly evanescence

I hand you a plate of lunatic fare;
crimson plums and ruby-red grief
remain our wish-fulfilling jewels

here's the food we forgot we had,
my hand cuts it open on your edge
and what was pity transforms
into a fugitive bird
flying from flower to flower, wanting to live
at least an hour longer

supper's ready
even if we are not

The Longest Suffering

Your depression
is doable.

A quip, a backrub,
a breath chasing the sun
down the spine
and then silence in place of
either correction or
sympathy.
Touching your shoulder
that is so sore
from the grand weight
your mind entrusts
to you
and me.

But anger?
I catch the fire
and we see
who can burn the house
down
first.

The God of Gaps

At the base
of tall redwoods
I stop thinking
about thinking.

I wait in the space
between tall words.

It's October and the late
afternoon light
rests on its side
yet wavers from the wind.

The wind's too much
for words I have remembered or found.
The only song now
is up in the crown.

There's room
between the song I want to hear
and what keeps singing up there.

There's a distance
between the right word
and me.

Sunlight diagonals
fall through tall pillars of spongy bark,
from canopy to duff,
to mark the link of shadow and light.
The trees invent the light.
They invite us to parse it.
We learn from what is sparse.

There is a Japanese word
for light like this
in the forest.

I can't remember it.
I can't remember enough.
Proper nouns, then nouns… in that order
words slow.
There is darkness between what I knew
and know.

The light in the forest
fills in its name,
komorebi.
Does this not sound like song?
Did it ever not sound like you
or me?

Nature needs to abhor a vacuum.
Without questions, words come
to the dark room between us.

The autumn wind
in this redwood forest can rain down
widowmakers in the gaps
or fill silence
with a rush of singing
or stain a page
with exactly the right word
as long as this light lasts

and joins us.

The Pitch Pipe

What's left of the brotherhood
wakes inside me,
the bell tuned to middle C
breaks the day open.

Habits are strong at dawn—
the ancient voices natter on.

Something surely is lost at night,
in the dreams willed to the living.
Every morning I wake to loss.

The sun and the sounds of morning
slam familiar doors. I need to move.
The mind remembers where it is,
and chugs into motion.

Although my work of making life
gets bogged down in boredom,
bugles blow to wake the dead.
And cosmogenesis and entropy
both clear their throats. The sound
of the universe self-creating does not fuck around.

But who am I kidding, I got kicked out of the Brotherhood
and I say good morning to coffee and self-cherishing,
my addictions of choice.
Losing the middle was exactly my heresy.

It's another morning of monkeys
left on my back, chipper in the cortex—
the chatter of the universe fixing its mistakes
off key, and amused by the filters awarded us.
And I just try to tell you about doors.

*

What I want to tell you is that loving these habits
opens doors. I want to tell you
that loss makes fullness.
Look at the world
that's left through
today's threshold.

In your throat
are green songs. And
black holes.
And a shrug
of the tired shelf-like shoulders.

Do a little stretching every morning.
Practice your scales.
Watch for falling branches.

And if you're in the mood
sing a green song stretching
across the inland sea.

*

The sailor and the friar in me
will at last embrace.
They learn at morning:
infinite darkness and eternal light
grow tall from one root,
flow from the same spring,
and both sing a song to forget limits.
And, oh, the root is not just theory.
My bones are a pitch pipe.
My throat, though passing,
whistles with what might have been possible.

Today begins.
A chord of choice
brought to me
by synapses and breath.

The anthem of the community
we kicked ourselves out of
sings in the bodies we have,
not the bodies
we lost in thought.

Today I'll practice scales
of heresy. From middle C
an octave stretches
asking to be sung
then sharpened by
capriccios and being
born again
into the community
of sentience.

An Apologia is not an Apology

The winds are so strong this morning.
Strong enough to blow

yellow sands and red earth off last night's words.
What at night was deeply buried

by morning emerges among these breezes.
I try to find the place

I committed the crime.
My grimy hands are clues—

they fold in faux remorse too close
to the dirty phonemes outlined in a coroner's chalk.

Blood clots on the hands where
the disease of burial cut them.

My scars, I guess, were wars against you.
Against your fleeting love, your exhaustion.

Now the wind has blown through
the chimera's marriage

joining heaven and hell. I threw
fragmentary sentences to wound you.

It was performance, my love,
not self-deception. I knew the midnight blue

lies would be found out in a golden dawn.
No doubt I hurled them anyway, striking deep.

Alchemical sleep
did not change a thing.

That redemption's out of reach.
Now as you walk into the kitchen

your eyes prepare coffee with scabs
on hands that will not forgive.

This morning the sky will not lie
for us, will not deny the fatal jabs.

As always, you eschew bandages
and do and do not care for these sober amends.

Oh, you will not talk.
And your silence is a megaphone.

All the colors remain on your side.
The winds of justice still darken mine.

What began last night
never ends. A game no one won,

and by refusing to be thought a fool
I became one.

Norwegian Wood

Are these not just excuses to not connect. Our differences are irrelevant. To only name the flaws. —Bjork

Perhaps it was wrong
to burn him in my bucket of ashes.
Perhaps raising fire
was only code for my incompetence.

He is a fine musician, he hears notes
better than words. I hear
the keys and chords of an unknown man
and my hunger looks for answers
in blue notes and echoes.

Words dry up. They always have.
But words are kindling too.

*

Sandalwood oil cools on the tabernacle of your wrist.
No sandalwood grew in Oslo.
Yet our little love nest on the fjord was full of sweet scent
and strong hot tea. I loved choosing furniture
for you. I loved dropping mint and sugar in your tea.
I loved singing a third above your melody.

You did not notice. You kept singing your lonely song.

*

How many tables did we construct?
How much experience can be stretched on them
now for examination? And how many conclusions
wow us then are moved like chess pieces?

The usual gambit
grabs your body from my memory
and I anele it with aloe and myrrh
as scripture demands. Ashes to ashes, you know.

So I clinch the white ash and a checkmate
from plane crashes, canals,
and ransomed songs foreshortened by history.
But the wooden hut we cobbled together
outlasts us. It outlasts even inept love.

The Open Hand Grasps S by the Neck

another morning
in deepest Tarturus
ices hands
on the tumbling marbled stone

after forgetful night
clenched darkness
in the frozen silver story
that swallowed his life;
                                        now, arctic winds
blow furling smoke
billowing to show
all the white filaments
of his regret.

it's not time. not yet.
he turns to check
old neighbors
with a manual light
teased into a tall tower.

the morning wakens
the mote round his skull.

and his eye empties the tides
to make space for the new dark cover
wedged in this, a final day.

his thinking is a white out.
he and all his neighbors
lose each other
in the foggy breath
of an alien world they choke on.

he straightens, grips the stone.
he was taught not to grasp the small
so he can grasp it all.

he stumbles pulling on silver shoes.

he needs to get started
or he'll perish in the beet-red mid-day heat ready to burn off
the stone, rolling back to his promise of sleep.

his hand presses flat on the Great Stone of his lying.

true fortune has no map, no lathe of stars
changing the route.

noon will burn with the fool's gold
and rotting fruit.

his dreams make neighbors,
his work is a scar of solitude.

only the open hand of first light
is true, all else is made to hide him.

he has learned not to grasp too tightly.

Tonight

The Teacher says
we must remember we will get old
feeble and die, and so if
we die tonight
have we no regrets. Though
I live in answers and invent suitable questions,
the Teacher's words are neither. They want
to free me from the screens
that eat our lives. The words offer maps
to meaning.

Tonight is coming. I wonder—
an aneurism in sleep would
be fine. Though I've thought
dying in one's sleep might also mean
waking
to pass alone, wandering off
into darkness
alone.

*

Today I hiked through a burned forest
with waves of ceanothus
and bush poppy surging in full-forced spring
on the ridge after showers
and the blackened poles of dead trees
pointing to the sky that was not the sky
for hours and hours.

I stopped, a "vista point", and ate
a square of cacao nibs, raw honey
sesame seed mash, and
            truffle oil?
it was packaged with serene graphics
and had melted in my pack, not
suitable at all for trail food. But
this trail through scarred and

reviving woods on steep slopes
whose rocks and ribs
finally saw the sun, didn't care.

Then I came home, showered and the old
cat jumped on the bed, purred for attention
and showed me her half-moon pink tongue
hanging out of her old mouth of missing teeth.

My husband has been far off
the last few days, though he types on
the sofa but two rooms away. His hard edges
and closed ears have weighed
like stones sent to Sisyphus.

But this is not the problem nor solution.
It's my mind that's sharpened his edges
and the weight I invent
soon plays in spring rain.

My mind
will stop looking for edges,
like it does.

Tonight, I'm ready. My heart too,
a pink half moon,
needs nothing more.

I guess stones suit me
and remorse washes away
as sleep comes.

Before Winter

A registered letter arrives. He tosses it on the laptop.
It's August, no need to open it yet, he reasons.

He wants to open the letter in time, with care.
He suspects seasons will fall out.

Spring, green and itchy.
Summer, sweaty and exhausting.

Fall, illuminating the body's sadness.
Winter, the deep unknowing skin.

He knows he's wrong about time—
now that the sunlight falls on its side.

He'll never make it to winter solstice,
but he pretends the days lengthen.

He rolls seasons up like sleeves,
and marches up his made-up hill.

He thinks the lie we all will tell is hard work.
We say it's a letter opener, but it's a murder weapon.

Then the letter opens on its own
and the days he does not live spill out.

A Reckoning

Old Sisyphus sets the table slowly. Guests are a big deal now.
The Librarian is coming for supper.
She'll bring the history of ideas.

It is late in the year and afternoon
so sunlight streams in acute angles through this room—
slow autumn light shines on dust motes rising like tired little angels.

Old S is tired too. The only stones he pushes now are in his kidney.
He stays inside for days and follows the shifting light
to see it change the room in endless afternoons; to see time fall.

Tonight, though, he'll meet her to settle effects and their causes.
He will admit to her he can't keep up at all.
Speed no longer feeds him and these hills are too steep.

At the head of this trestle table he'll place human error.
That'll be his chair where they'll negotiate the death they share
and then map how the mortal mind always misses the point.

She'll come at sunset, her arms loaded with scrolls—
long lists of appeals, old stipulations,
a faulty memory, and lives of purpose scribed on parchments.

He knows what she'll ask of him when she comes.
she'll ask him to free them from his needy heart's ache.

*

There in the corner of the dining room wait
papers he'll show her. The bloodwork from the lab,
under a cucurbit of dried mushrooms and madrone twigs.

And the overdue book on Plotinus he promised
to return to her. She'll forgive him.
She always does. It is her act. A dance of withered figs.

Now he hears her hooves scratch at the door.
His best and last offer will be to open it. He takes a breath
to prepare himself for the curse of silence they'll explore.

His wobble shames him. His unbalance bores her.
Oh his wrinkled cherished hand smooths his hair
then opens the polished door to see her there.

*

He could ask her to dance,
but he won't.

He could offer drinks from the river of consolation
but he won't.

So they will hold each other
until they don't.

There is work to do. Even ancient trees live to produce fruit.
They exhaust the light on this longest of nights.

Every idea waits for them, patient as blood.
Then she wraps a spell around the philosopher's stone.

She points to where he sits and says, "if this makes you feel special,
dismiss it. Not even your mistakes are real."

He thinks she sounds like his mother, the punishment and calcination.
His origin is in her and what's left of fire passes from one life

to another. At last they scratch at their saddle of human aspiration
and lie to each other like husband and wife.

But it is an accounting, not love, she came for. The books are closed.
The parchments rolled out nothing but dust and mold.

This poem, this skin of utterance, is an impermanent fool,
and all fools die, turn to stone, and roll down

the mountain. The mountain where epithets huddle
making plans for his surrender. S agrees to these cold terms.

So done and signed, she rings the bells. Work is over.
Now she is his dream to wake from,

with a stone on his tongue.
The new ash will make an earth in his sleep.
And the season of sleep finally here.

HR Harper lives in the redwoods above Santa Cruz CA with a partner, two good dogs, and a cranky cat. He was a creative writing major at UCLA, studying with Jascha Kessler and Cal Bedient, and then studied in the English Ph.D. program there. He then worked as an educator in central city schools in Southern and Northern California for many years. He got a couple masters and then a doctorate in education from UCSC, with a focus on immigrant integration.

He's also long been a student of the emptying traditions, which inform his writing. He writes to understand human consciousness in a natural world humans (and their invented devices) seem to be destroying. Writing poetry and fiction for years, he began to publish in 2021. Some of his recently published poems and fiction may be found at: https://brusheswiththedarklaw.blogspot.com/

www.ingramcontent.com/pod-product-compliance
Lightning Source LLC
LaVergne TN
LVHW091814110826
845146LV00006B/1236

* 9 7 9 8 8 9 9 9 0 4 5 3 0 *